DATE DUE   MAY   2014

Score
with
Race Car Math

Stuart A. P. Murray

Enslow Elementary
an imprint of
Enslow Publishers, Inc.
40 Industrial Road
Box 398
Berkeley Heights, NJ 07922
USA

http://www.enslow.com

Enslow Elementary, an imprint of Enslow Publishers, Inc.
Enslow Elementary® is a registered trademark of Enslow Publishers, Inc.

Library of Congress Cataloging-in-Publication Data

Murray, Stuart, 1948-
  Score with race car math / Stuart A. P. Murray.
      pages cm. — (Score with sports math)
  Includes index.
  Summary: "Get fun race car facts while practicing math techniques used in racing sports such as figuring out
averages. Also includes math problem-solving tips"—Provided by publisher.
  ISBN 978-0-7660-4177-6
  1. Race Cars—Mathematics—Juvenile literature. I. Title.
  GV1029.9.S74 2014
  796.720151—dc23

                            2012028797

Future editions:
Paperback ISBN: 978-1-4644-0293-7   EPUB ISBN: 978-1-4645-1183-7
Single-User PDF ISBN: 978-1-4646-1183-4   Multi-User PDF ISBN: 978-0-7660-5812-5

Printed in China
012013 Leo Paper Group, Heshan City, Guangdong, China
10 9 8 7 6 5 4 3 2 1

To Our Readers: We have done our best to make sure all Internet Addresses in this book were active and
appropriate when we went to press. However, the author and the publisher have no control over and assume no
liability for the material available on those Internet sites or on other Web sites they may link to. Any comments
or suggestions can be sent by e-mail to comments@enslow.com or to the address on the back cover.

Design and Production: Rachel D. Turetsky, Lily Book Productions

Illustration Credits: Action Sports Photography/Shutterstock.com, pp. 24 (top), 27, 28 (top), 28 (bottom),
31, 32, 35 (top), 36, 42, 45; Beelde Photography/Shutterstock.com, p. 34; Boomer544/Photos.com, p. 4;
carroteater/Shutterstock.com, p. 18 (bottom); Danshutter/Shutterstock.com, p. 1; David Acosta Allely/Shutterstock.
com, p. 20; iStockphoto.com/Adrian Thomas, pp. 31 (bottom), 44; iStockphoto.com/chrysh, p. 33 (top);
iStockphoto.com/derausdo, p. 15; iStockphoto.com/Jello5700, p. 18 (top); iStockphoto.com/maomage, p. 6
(left); iStockphoto.com/matt_scherf, p. 37; Library of Congress Prints and Photographs Division, Washington,
D.C., pp. 8 (bottom), 11, 13; mart/Shutterstock.com, pp. 24 (bottom), 25; Marynchenko Oleksandr/
Shutterstock.com, p. 35 (center); Murphylgor/Shutterstock.com, p. 26; Natykach Nataliia/Shutterstock.com,
p. 17; nobrand121876/Shutterstock.com, p. 33 (bottom); notkoo/Shutterstock.com, pp. 31 (bottom), 35
(bottom); Randesya Archam Irdani/Shutterstock.com, p. 3; RATOCA/Shutterstock.com, pp. 6 (right), 44;
Rick Lewis/Shutterstock.com, p. 25; Roberto Cerruti/Shutterstock.com, p. 8 (top); Wikimedia/State Archives
of Florida, Florida Memory, http://floridamemory.com/items/show/33539, p. 14; U.S. Air Force photo by Larry
McTighe, p. 7; Wikimedia/Indianapolis Motor Speedway, p. 16; Wikimedia/Darryl Moran, p. 43; Wikimedia/
English Steel Corp., p. 22 (top); Wikimedia/Glen Duncombe, p. 46; Wikimedia/Holger Behr, p. 10; Wikimedia/
Ian McWilliams, p. 22 (bottom); Wikimedia/Morven, p. 30; Wikimedia/Rob Clenshaw, p. 38 (bottom); Wikimedia/
Royalbroil, p. 38 (top); Wikimedia/*Scientific American* (1896), p. 5; Wikimedia/the359, p. 21; Wikimedia/Will
Pittenger, p. 41.

Cover Photo: Lisa Norman-Hudson/Associated Press

Contents

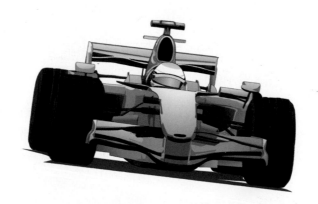

A single-seat race car speeds along on a race track.

INTRODUCTION
Race Cars and Car Races

Ever since the first automobile, drivers have raced to see whose car is fastest. Even back in the 1800s, when the fastest cars were run by steam, drivers raced them. Steam was the same force that powered mighty train engines.

In the 1800s, steam automobiles were joined by gasoline-powered cars designed for use on roads. Both types were called "horseless carriages." They were slower than four-horse stagecoaches or one-horse carriages. The power of the automobile

4

was measured against the strength of horses. Early cars only had the power of three horses: three horsepower (hp). Automobiles improved in speed and power, but most roads were only dirt tracks. Driving on them was bumpy and slow. When cars broke down, people riding by in carriages laughed and shouted, "Get a horse!"

Horseless carriages to 700 horsepower

Automobile designs and engines developed rapidly. In the early twentieth century, most cars were large and heavy. They were meant for driving over rocky roads and through mud.

Most cars only went 35 to 40 miles an hour, but auto races were still exciting. Cars racing at the local horse track became a favorite event for people everywhere in America.

"Horseless carriages" prepare for the start of a race in 1896.

Roads and race tracks improved, and "motoring" caught on around the world. Cars became faster and more comfortable. Buyers wanted the models that won the big races. Manufacturers could show off their vehicles in those races, so they organized more of them. Modern race tracks now had hard surfaces instead of dirt. Race cars became more powerful, until some went over 300 miles an hour. The strongest engines now had 700 horsepower. Auto racing was more thrilling than ever.

In this book, you'll learn some auto-racing facts and history, and you'll practice math, too. Knowing math makes auto racing even more exciting.

A worldwide spectator sport

There are many types of auto racing. The most popular races are stock car, Formula One, and dragsters. Other races include dirt track, sport car, go-kart, pickup truck, and races by solar-powered and electric vehicles.

Some cars race around oval tracks a couple of miles long. Others zoom down short drag strips. Many race in "rallies" along winding roads and across hundreds of miles of rugged countryside. Auto racing is one of the world's most popular sports, with the big races seen by millions of spectators in more than 200 countries.

Stock cars at Daytona International Speedway.

Top: A restored 1925 Bugatti race car competes in a long distance *race* in 2011. Bottom: Joe *Daw*son drives a National to win the 1912 Indianapolis *500*.

1

Speed: King of the Race Track

By the early 1900s, inventors and mechanics around the world were building cars that were going faster and faster. In 1906, a steam-powered car rocketed along a Florida beach at more than 127 mph.

At first most races were more about going long distances than about speed. The longest car race ever was in 1908: 22,000 miles, from New York to Paris.

In 1909, the race that would become the Indianapolis 500 was first held before a crowd of 40,000 cheering fans. On oval-shaped tracks, speed was king.

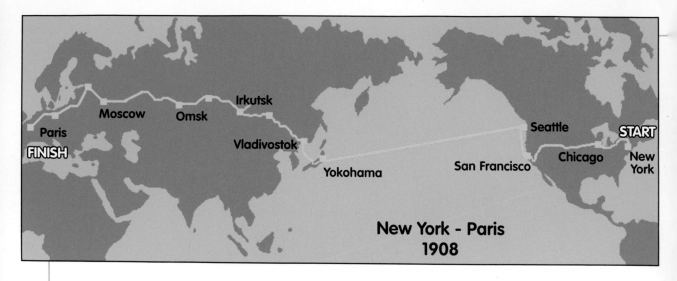

Irkutsk
Moscow   Omsk
Paris   Vladivostok   Seattle   START
FINISH   New
                              Yokohama   San Francisco   Chicago   York

New York - Paris
1908

The longest auto race of all

In 1908, Americans driving the "Thomas Flyer"
won the New York to Paris auto race in exactly
169 days. The Flyer first crossed the United States
to the Pacific Ocean in 41 days, 8 hours, and 15
minutes. The journey continued by ship, then
on land to Paris.

Q: After crossing the United States, how much
   longer did it take the Flyer to reach Paris?
   Round off to the nearest day.

A: Round off 41 days, 8 hours, and 15 minutes:
   41 days
   Subtract 41 days from 169 days:
   169 − 41 = 128 days

There were six teams: American, Italian, German, and three French. They fought sandstorms, blizzards, desert heat, mud, and breakdowns. Only three made it: the Americans, Italians, and Germans.

The cars in Times Square for the start of the race. The U.S. car is not in the picture.

Q: The Flyer arrived 26 days ahead of the second-place Italians. How many days did the Italians take?

A: Add 26 days to 169 days:

169 + 26 = 195 days

The Flyer left New York on February 12 at 11:15 in the morning and reached Paris on July 26 at 6:15 in the evening.

Q: What time was it in New York?

A: It took exactly 169 days, no hours or minutes, so in New York it was the same time as the race started: 11:15 in the morning.

Horsepower and miles per hour

The first cars had the power of three or four horses (hp). They could go only a few miles an hour (mph). Wisconsin offered $10,000 to builders of the first car that could go 5 mph for 200 miles. Modern cars have the power of hundreds of horses and can go more than 100 mph.

Q: An early car had a top speed of 5 mph. How fast is a modern car that is 30 times faster?

A: Multiply the early car's 5 mph by 30:

$30 \times 5 = 150$

The modern car can go 150 mph.

The first American auto race was in Illinois in 1895. The winning car was called a "motorized wagon." It took over 10 hours to go 54 miles.

Q: What was the car's speed in mph?

A: Divide 54 miles by 10 hours:

$54 \div 10 = 5.4$

The car's speed was 5.4 mph.

A "motorized wagon" built by brothers Charles (pictured) and J. Frank Duryea won the 1895 Illinois race. It was the first American car to use gasoline.

Q: A top racehorse can run a mile in 2 minutes. What is its mph?

A: Find how many miles the horse would cover in 60 minutes (1 hour).

Divide 60 minutes by 2 minutes:

$60 \div 2 = 30$

The racehorse is going 30 mph (30 miles in one hour).

The Stanley Rocket sets the speed record at Daytona Beach, Florida.

Rocket and the racehorse

In 1906, the steam-powered Stanley Steamer Rocket race car set the world land speed record. The Rocket's speed was 127.69 miles per hour.

Q: Round the Rocket's speed to the closest mile per hour.

A: 127.69 rounds up to 128 miles per hour.

Q: At 128 miles per hour, how many miles would the Rocket travel in three hours?

A: Multiply 128 by 3:

128 x 3 = 384 miles

Q: About how many seconds did the Rocket take to cover one mile? (There are 3,600 seconds in an hour.)

A: Divide 128 mph into 3,600 seconds:

3,600 ÷ 128 = 28.13 seconds per mile

The Rocket went a mile in about 28 seconds.

Q: How many times faster was the Rocket than the racehorse's 30 mph? Round to the nearest whole number.

A: Divide 128 mph by 30 mph:

128 ÷ 30 = 4.27

4.27 rounds to 4.

The Rocket was 4 times faster than the horse.

This cockpit of an early race car has a clock and a speed gauge.

The First Indy 500

When the Indianapolis Motor Speedway first opened in 1909, there were two races: 250 miles and 300 miles. In 1911, there was one race of 500 miles: the Indy 500.

Q: If a driver completed both Indy races in 1909, how far did he go?

A: Add 250 miles and 300 miles:

$$250 + 300 = 550 \text{ miles}$$

The Indianapolis Motor Speedway is shown just before it first opened in 1909.

Q: How much farther was a 500-mile race than the 200 miles Wisconsin had called for?

A: Subtract 200 miles from 500 miles:

500 − 200 = 300 miles farther.

Q: In 1911, Ray Harroun won the first Indy 500 going 15 times the 5 mph speed Wisconsin had called for. How fast did he go?

A: Multiply 5 times 15:

5 × 15 = 75 mph

Q: The 1912 first prize (or purse) was $50,000. That's twice as much as it was in 1911. How much was the purse in 1911?

A: Divide $50,000 by 2:

50,000 ÷ 2 = 25,000

The 1911 purse was $25,000.

2

Open-Wheel Race Cars

Every May, more than 400,000 auto racing fans come to the Indy 500, the greatest race for open-wheel Indy cars.

"Open-wheel" means the wheels are outside the car's body. Indy cars have their own design and engines. So do Formula One cars, which are also open-wheel. Formula One races are often called Grand Prix.

Open-wheel cars are the fastest speedway and road cars in the world. They can race for hours at speeds of 170–230 mph—if they do not break down or crash. Drivers of open-wheel race cars have top driving skills and cool courage.

A close battle for the lead at the Indy 500.
Inset: A pit crew in action at the Indy 500.

Indy cars and Formula One

The Indy car design is similar to the Formula One (F1) race car design. They are both single-seaters (one driver), have open wheels, and are low to the ground. Indy cars and F1 cars reach speeds of 220 mph or more.

Q: The first Indy 500 race in 1911 had 40 cars. All but one had both a driver and mechanic. How many people were in that first race?

A: Since one car only had a driver, multiply 40 times 2 and subtract 1:

40 × 2 = 80

80 − 1 = 79 total drivers and mechanics

A Formula One races at a track in Spain.

Cars at the Indy 500 start in a grid. The top drivers take the front positions.

Today, the Indy 500 has 33 cars, and they start the race set up in "grids" of 3 cars each.

Q: How many "grids" are there at the start?
A: Divide 33 by 3:

$33 \div 3 = 11$ grids

Of the 400,000 fans who come to see the Indy 500 at the Indianapolis Motor Speedway, 257,000 have seats in the grandstand. The rest are mostly on the infield grass inside the track.

Q: How many Indy fans are in the infield during the race?
A: Subtract 257,000 from 400,000:

$400,000 - 257,000 = 143,000$ fans

Left: Graham Hill is the only Indy 500 winner (1966) to win the "Triple Crown of Motorsport." This also includes the Monaco Grand Prix, an F1 race, and the 24 Hours of Le Mans, a sport car race. Below: Grandson Josh Hill races Hill's Indy-winning car.

Worldwide auto racing fans

Formula One cars race in many countries. Indy cars race mainly in the United States. Before 1923 all Indy 500 cars had to have a driver and a mechanic in the car during the race. Since few cars had rearview mirrors, the mechanic had to warn the driver when cars were trying to pass.

Q: As car design improved, Indy 500 cars were allowed to have just a driver. That was 23 years before the first F1 race. What year was that first F1 race?

A: Add 1923 and 23:

1923 + 23 = 1946, the first F1 race

Q: The worldwide television audience for the Indy 500 is 6.8 million. Write 6.8 million as a number and then in words:

A: 6,800,000

Six million eight hundred thousand

Q: Formula One championship races have a worldwide television audience of 600 million in 200 countries. What is the average number of viewers per country?

A: Divide 600 million by 200:

600 million ÷ 200 = 3 million viewers

The F1 speed record of 257 mph was set in 2005. The Indy car speed record of 256.948 mph was set in 1996.

Q: Round off the Indy car speed to the closest mph and find out which was faster.

A: 256.948 rounds to 257 mph.

Their record speeds are the same.

Pit crew members finish and jump clear so this stock car can get back in the race.

Drivers and pit crews

Each driver is part of a racing team. Some on the team design, build, and test drive the car. Before the race, a test driver often makes "qualifying" laps around the race track to show the car is fast enough to enter.

Q: Indy 500 cars do 4 qualifying laps totaling 10 miles. How long is each lap?

A: Divide 10 by 4:

$10 \div 4 = 2.5$

An Indy lap is 2.5 miles long.

A racing team must have fast "pit crews." Cars make "pit stops," and crews of 5–20 quickly refuel, make repairs, check the engine, and change tires. The faster the pit crew, the sooner the car gets back in the race.

Q: During a 500-mile race a car makes 5 pit stops averaging 12 seconds each. How much total time has the car lost?

A: First, ignore the 500 miles, which is extra information. Multiply 5 pit stops times an average of 12 seconds:

5 × 12 = 60 seconds lost

Nine women have driven in the Indy 500. Janet Guthrie was the first woman to enter the race, in 1977. The best finish was Danica Patrick's third place in 2009.

Q: How many years after Guthrie did Patrick win third?

A: Subtract 1977 from 2009:

2009 − 1977 = 32 years

Danica Patrick is the most successful female open-wheel racing driver.

The Indy's first century

In the more than one hundred years of Indy 500s, there have been 96 races and 67 winners (through 2012). Three drivers share the record for the most wins: A.J. Foyt, Al Unser, and Rick Mears all had four wins.

Most Victories

Foyt: 1961, 1964, 1967, 1977

Unser: 1970, 1971, 1978, 1987

Mears: 1979, 1984, 1988, 1991

Q: Only five drivers have won the Indy two years in a row. Study the Most Victories chart to see whether any of those drivers won twice in a row.

A: Unser won two years in a row, 1970 and 1971.

2011 winner Dan Wheldon won 102.4 times the $25,000 purse won by Harroun in the 1911 Indy.

Q: Round 102.4 to the
   nearest hundred and
   estimate Wheldon's purse.
A: 102.4 rounds off to 100.
   Multiply 25,000 by 100:
   25,000 × 100 = 2,500,000
   (The actual 2011 purse
   was $2.56 million.)

Dan Wheldon won
the 2011 Indy.

The record for the fastest average speed was
made in 1990 by Arie Luyendyk: 186 mph.

Q: How many times faster is Luyendyk's speed
   than Ray Harroun's 75 mph in 1911?
A: Divide 186 by 75:
   186 ÷ 75 = 2.48
   Almost two and a half times faster!

Q: And how many times faster is it than the
   5 mph speed Wisconsin gave a prize for in the
   late 1800s?
A: Divide 186 by 5:
   186 ÷ 5 = 37.2 times faster!

Top: The bodies of Funny Car drag racers are raised for inspection.
Bottom: Jamie McMurray does a "burnout" to celebrate his NASCAR win.

3

Stock Cars, Dragsters, and Rallies

Stock cars look like super-hot "street cars," but they are designed for speed and handling. Speeds can top 200 mph as they race around oval or twisting tracks, fighting for the lead. Stock car races are under the National Association for Stock Car Auto Racing (NASCAR).

The fastest race cars are the dragsters, which can go 330 mph. Drag racers peel out for short distances and have to be stopped by a parachute opening behind them. Road rallies are races for several days over long distances. Rallies can include public roads, open countryside, jungles, and even river crossings.

Stock cars get faster

By the 1930s, stock cars meant cars from the "stock" of carmakers who sold to the public. In the 1950s, a Chrysler was called the C-300 because of its 300 hp engine. It was said to be "the world's fastest stock car," with a speed of 127 mph.

Q: In 2012 some NASCAR race cars had 750 hp and speeds over 230 mph. Which has increased more since that C-300, hp or mph?

A: Find how many times more are modern hp and mph.

Divide 750 by 300 and 230 by 127:

$750 \div 300 = 2.5$ times more hp

$230 \div 127 = 1.8$ times mph

2.5 is larger than 1.8

Horsepower has increased more than speed.

The Chrysler C-300 was a high-performance luxury car used in stock car races.

Cars round a turn in a NASCAR Sprint Cup race at Daytona Speedway.

The C-300 was made about 60 years before the 2012 Sprint Cup car. By the year 2072, stock cars might again increase their hp 2.5 times and mph 1.8 times.

Q: What might the Sprint Cup car's hp and mph be in 2072?

A: Multiply 750 by 2.5 and 230 by 1.8:

750 × 2.5 = 1,875 hp

230 × 1.8 = 414 mph

Cars enter the New Hampshire Motor Speedway track for a Sprint Cup Series race.

NASCAR racing

NASCAR has more than 1,500 stock car races on 100 tracks in the United States every year. There are 36 races every year in NASCAR's Sprint Cup Series, which is the most popular group of stock car races.

Q: What is the average number of NASCAR races per track?

A: Divide 1,500 races by 100 tracks:

   1,500 ÷ 100 = 150 races per track

Q: What fraction of 1,500 is 150?

A: $^{150}/_{1500}$

Reduce the fraction by dividing the numerator and denominator by 150:

$150 \div 150 = 1$

$1,500 \div 150 = 10$

$^1/_{10}$ is the fraction.

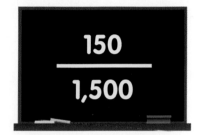

Sprint Cup drivers earn points if they get first place, second place, or third place in the races they enter. They also get points for every lap they lead during races.

Q: In a 200-lap race, driver A led half the laps and driver B led one quarter of the laps. How many laps did each driver lead?

A: To find half the laps, divide 200 by 2:

$200 \div 2 = 100$ laps (Driver A)

To find one quarter of the laps, divide 200 by 4:

$200 \div 4 = 50$ laps (Driver B)

Speed and distance

Stock cars can reach speeds of 200 mph, but they are heavier than open-wheel race cars. That means they do not handle as well on curves. When racing on an oval track, stock cars go 70 percent as fast as open-wheel race cars.

Q: If an Indy car can do 200 mph on an oval track, how fast would a stock car go on that same track?

A: Since stock cars go 70 percent as fast, find 70 percent of 200 mph.

70 percent is the same as .70, or .7

Multiply .7 times 200:

.7 × 200 = 140.0

The stock car would do 140 mph.

The red car stays in the "draft" of the lead car at Charlotte Motor Speedway. "Drafting" helps pull the red car forward and saves gas.

This aerial view shows the Bristol Motor Speedway in Tennessee.

Some stock car race tracks are one quarter of a mile long. Others are two and six tenths miles long.

Q: Express the two track lengths in fractions and then in decimals.

A: One quarter = $\frac{1}{4}$ and .25

Two and six tenths = $2\frac{6}{10}$ and 2.6

Q: Which stock car race is longer: 200 laps on a 2-mile track or 600 laps on a quarter-mile track?

A: Multiply 200 laps by 2 miles:

200 × 2 = 400 miles

We can find a quarter of a number by dividing by 4.

Divide 600 laps by 4:

600 ÷ 4 = 150 miles

The 200-lap race is longer.

A parachute opens to slow down this dragster.

Drag strips and rallying

Drag racing is short and explosive. Some drag racers have huge rear tires and pointed front ends. They are built for speed over short, straight distances. Rally races are long and grinding. Cars in rallies have to survive bad weather, country roads, and mechanical problems.

Q: A dragster races down a strip of 1,000 feet in 3.8 seconds. How many feet per second did the dragster go (to the nearest tenth)?

A: Divide 1,000 by 3.8:

1,000 ÷ 3.8 = 263.2 ft. per second.

Q: How many seconds (to the nearest tenth) would that drag racer need to go a football field 300 ft. long?

A: Divide 300 feet by 263.2 ft. per second:
300 ÷ 263.2 = 1.1 seconds to go the length of the field.

Position	1	2	3	4	5	6	7	8	9	10
Points	20	15	12	10	8	6	4	3	2	1

Rallies give points to the first 10 finishers in each stage.

Rally racing is done in stages over long distances. Cars win points by how they finish in each stage.

Q: In the rally on the chart, how many points does a car earn if it is 1st twice, 2nd once, 9th three times, and 10th once?

A: Figure the points for each place and add them together.
1st: 2 × 20 = 40, 2nd: 15,
9th: 3 × 2 = 6, 10th: 1
40 + 15 + 6 + 1 = 62 points

Rally cars must be "street legal," although they often race in deserts and on mountain roads.

4

Daytona 500: NASCAR's Top Sprint Cup Race

In 1998, Dale Earnhardt was one of the best NASCAR drivers of all time. In a career of 24 years, Earnhardt had won more than 70 races and 7 national championships. But what he wanted most was to win the Daytona 500. He had failed 19 times before to win this famous NASCAR race.

The Daytona 500 is held at Florida's Daytona International Speedway. It is the best-known NASCAR Sprint Cup Race and is called "The Great American Race."

These were Dale Earnhardt's stock cars.

"The Great American Race"

Dale Earnhardt came to Daytona with the aim to win America's most popular car race. Daytona's television audience is 35.5 million, while the Indy 500 has 6.8 million.

Q: How much larger is Daytona's U.S. television audience?

A: Subtract 6.8 million from 35.5 million:

$$35.5 - 6.8 = 28.7 \text{ million}$$

The Daytona 500 has 28.7 million more viewers.

The Daytona 500 starts 43 drivers who race 500 miles in 200 laps. In 2012 the winner earned $1,590,000. The 1959 winner's purse was $19,000.

Q: About how many times larger was the 2012 purse?

A: Divide $1,590,000 by $19,000 (First, take away the last three zeros of each number):

$$1,590 \div 19 = 83.68$$

The 2012 purse was about 83.68 times larger.

The Daytona track is 2.5 miles long and in a tri-oval. This shape makes it easier for race fans to see the cars on the track.

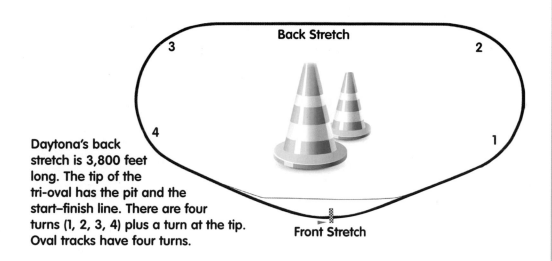

Daytona's back stretch is 3,800 feet long. The tip of the tri-oval has the pit and the start–finish line. There are four turns (1, 2, 3, 4) plus a turn at the tip. Oval tracks have four turns.

Q: Look at the shape of the track. What two geometric figures can be seen in this shape?

A: The tri-oval combines a triangle and oval.

Q: Earnhardt drives 200 mph and covers almost 300 ft. per second. How many seconds will he take to do the 3,800-ft. back stretch?

A: Divide 3,800 by 300 (First take away the last two zeros):

38 ÷ 3 = 12.7 seconds

Earnhardt and Petty

Earnhardt's seven NASCAR championships tied him with Richard Petty, the greatest stock car driver of all.

Q: Earnhardt won championships in 7 of his 24 years as a driver. What percent of those 24 years was he champion?

A: Divide 24 into 7:

$$7 \div 24 = .29$$

$$.29 = 29 \text{ percent}$$

In 1959, Richard Petty's father, Lee Petty, won the first-ever Daytona. Richard won the Daytona seven times, which is the record. His last win was in 1981.

Richard Petty visits Daytona in 2010, soon after entering NASCAR's Hall of Fame.

Dale Earnhardt in
the late 1990s.

Q: Richard Petty was the first driver to win
Daytona in three different decades. What were
the three decades? (Remember, his last win
was in 1981.)

A: Figure the decades backwards: 1980s, 1970s,
and 1960s.

Another of Petty's Daytona records was the
most years between a driver's first and last victory:
17 years.

Q: What year was Petty's first win?

A: Subtract 17 years from 1981:

$1981 - 17 = 1964$

1964 was Petty's first Daytona win.

Richard Petty also held the Daytona record for
leading the most laps in a race: 184, set in 1964.

The Pettys also held two special records: Richard had the largest winning margin—two full laps (5 miles) ahead of the second-place car. Lee had the smallest winning margin, just 2 feet.

Q: Two Daytona laps are 26,400 feet. How much more is this than Lee's 2-foot margin?

A: Subtract 2 feet from 26,400 feet:

26,400 − 2 = 26,398 feet

A 20th try for victory

Dale Earnhardt had completed the Daytona 500 race 13 times. That was the record. Could he make it 14?

Q: How many total miles are in 14 races?

A: Multiply 500 miles by 14:

500 × 14 = 7,000 miles

Earnhardt drove all-out and led 107 of the 200 laps. With cars right behind him, he held on for victory. Earnhardt's average lap speed was 172.7 mph, the third fastest ever at Daytona.

Q: Earnhardt's speed was just 4.9 mph slower than the record set by Buddy Baker in 1980. What was Baker's speed?

A: Add 172.7 and 4.9:

172.7 + 4.9 = 177.6 is Baker's record

Q: How many more laps did Petty lead (184) in 1964 than Earnhardt led in 1998?

A: Subtract Earnhardt's 107 laps from Petty's 184:

184 − 107 = 77 laps

No matter how many records Richard Petty held, Dale Earnhardt finally had won the Daytona 500!

U.S. jet fighters demonstrate flying in formation for the auto racing crowd at Daytona.

Math Problem-Solving Tips

✎ Always read the problem completely before beginning to work on it.

✎ Make sure you understand the question.

✎ Some problems take more than one step to find the final answer.

✎ Don't think you always have to use every number in the problem. Some numbers are extra information that are not needed for the calculations.

✎ If you know your answer is wrong but can't find the mistake, then start again on a clean sheet of paper.

✎ Don't get upset! You can solve problems better when you're calm.

✎ If you're stuck on a problem, skip it and go on with the rest of them. You can come back to it.

Further Reading

Books

American Education Publishing. *The Complete Book of Math, Grades 3 and 4*. Greensboro, N.C.: Carson-Dellosa Publishing Publishing, 2009.

Connolly, Sean. *The Book of Perfectly Perilous Math*. New York: Workman Publishing Company, 2012.

Fitzgerald, Theresa. *Math Dictionary for Kids*. Waco, Tex.: Prufrock Press, Inc., 2011.

Web Sites

Drexel University. The Math Forum @ Drexel University
<http://www.mathforum.org/k12/mathtips>
K–12 math problems, puzzles, and tips and tricks.

IXL Learning © 2012 IXL Learning.
<http://www.ixl.com>
Math practice of all kinds, through interactive games and practice that make math practice fun.

Index